SO YOU WANT TO BECOME A PARK RANGER?

SO YOU WANT TO BECOME A PARK RANGER?

GETTING THE JOB; SETTING YOUR GOALS; EXPERIENCING THE "WEALTH"

RICHARD BOYER

This book was printed in the United States of America.

To order additional copies of this book, contact:
Xlibris Corporation
1-888-795-4274
www.Xlibris.com
Orders@Xlibris.com
73857

CONTENTS

*Rocky Mountain National Park

This book is dedicated, first of all, to my wife Dorothy, who has supported me throughout this post-retirement profession, not only with unconditional encouragement, but also by accompanying me to several of the sites, supporting me and the other staff members, while providing her hand-made cinnamon rolls to staff meetings and to various staff members. At the Lincoln Home National Historic Site, she received the "ISWYD" (I saw what you did) award for providing these always-delicious pastries. Secondly, the dedication is to our four children and their spouses—Mike and Nancy, Mark and Mary, Jim and La, and Beverly. All have provided support in a variety of ways. Finally, are the supportive and inspiring bosses, fellow rangers and other staff I have had the opportunity to work with at the various National Park Service units.

THANKS

Many thanks to the following people who have provided support, advice and inspiration for my work as a seasonal interpretative park ranger: Sue Langdon, Mary Wilson, Carol McBryant, LaShelle Lyman, Jean Muenchrath, Leanne Benton, Joan Childers, Kathy Brown, Judy Visty, Jeff Maugans, David Blackburn, Gene Finke, Cat Mancusco, Lynda Mealue, Heidi Weinert, John Golda, Kathy Daskal, Don Miller, John Gunn, Larry Frederick, Dick Putney, Kathy Edwards and Kathleen Kelly.

INTRODUCTION

It has been one my life's pleasures to work several years as a seasonal interpretative park ranger, park guide or education technician for the National Park Service.

The service has provided me with an outstanding retirement profession, personal satisfaction, and a chance to interact with outstanding people—both other staff and the visiting public.

The various staffs, without exception, have been dedicated, helpful, and passionate, committed to making visitor experiences meaningful, educational, and inspiring.

Millions of people visit our National Park Service units every year. They possess characteristics of love of nature, history, and culture. Almost, without exception, they have shown respect to the service and to the staff.

This book should provide a guide to those who want to enter the service. I have worked seasonally for 16 years at the following parks: Rocky Mountain National Park in Colorado, Redwood National and State Parks in California, Point Reyes National Seashore in California, the Lincoln Home National Historic Site in Illinois, and John Muir National Historic Site in California.

This book will discuss seeking and applying for a position; nuts and bolts of arriving; preparing before and on the job; but most importantly, what the job can bring to you.

The joys and sometimes the sorrows will make up the major part of the book, and hopefully will inspire many to seek employment in one of the most exciting and inspirational positions in the world!

NATIONAL PARK SERVICE MISSION STATEMENT

The National Park Service mission is to conserve the scenery and the natural and historic objects and the wildlife therein and to provide for the same in such manner and by such means as will leave them unimpaired for the enjoyment of future generations.

—Organic Act, 1916

FORWARD

As all seasonal interpretative rangers and guides must do, a theme, goals, and objectives must be developed which define each program they do for a position. This has been done here.

Theme: To work for the National Park Service, means that the person will embrace the service with patience, enthusiasm, and inspiration.

Goals:
Working for the park service means:

1. Being patient as you search and wait for a position.
2. Bringing enthusiasm for the job, for the resource, and for park visitors.
3. Being inspired by the resource and passing that inspiration to others.

Objectives:
By the end of this book, the reader will:

1. Understand how to get a job with the National Park Service.
2. Assess in writing his/her personal and professional enthusiasm and list three ways to bring that enthusiasm to the park service.
3. List three ways of being inspired by the resource.

SEEKING AND FINDING A JOB

Many visitors will ask what it takes to become a park ranger. They will ask what training you need, how you apply, and how you are assigned to a park—all good questions.

Competition is high with many people of all ages seeking positions, sometimes as many as 300 applying for just a few openings.

It took me three years, after submitting several applications back in the early 90's, before being offered a job at Rocky Mountain National Park—as a park ranger, (now called Visitor Use Assistant) GS-3—working as a fee collector at the Beaver Meadows Entrance Station. Mary, the hiring official, put her faith in me, which helped me begin this new second profession. Some of the experiences will be revealed later. Mary checked at least two references—one an Estes Park store manager where I had worked for three summers, and the other was the volunteer coordinator at the Ronald Reagan Home in Dixon, IL where I had served as a volunteer guide for two years. Incidentally, any volunteer work as a guide or docent in a historic site or park seems helpful.

Working three summers as a park policeman at Lowell Park in Dixon IL and ten years as a special deputy for the Lee County Sheriff's Department in Illinois seemed helpful.

The employment form, at that time, consisted of filling in bubbles, much like a standardized test. It took at least a couple of hours to fill in the bubbles with information including personal information, colleges and universities attended, courses taken, and jobs. And, you got to do this with each position you were applying for! It is much easier now with an on-line site, allowing you to put your resume on-line, and to send it on-line to the parks where you are applying or to fax your resume. Some parks still require you to send your resume in a prescribed manner—that is, with specific information requested from that park. Often, written answers to that position's knowledge, skills, and abilities (KSA's) are required. Almost every park will have slightly different KSA's; some will not require any. I keep a current resume and current KSA's on the computer. Sometimes you can adjust the KSA's to fit another job.

The web site you can use is *www.usajobs.opm.gov* Jobs are posted on-line, sometimes for just a few days, other times for two, three or more weeks. So, almost any day, you may find a new listing. You will have until the announcement closing date to submit all materials to the selected park. I urge you to check weekly for job openings. Also, jobs are listed several weeks or months ahead of the expected start date. Many winter jobs are listed as early as June or July; summer jobs are often listed as early as December or January. Don't wait to submit your applications until just before a season starts.

People sometimes come in after a season starts and want to know how to get a current job at the park. It is too late, unless there is an emergency hire going on.

Some hints that might help you get that job would be advice I received from others. Jim, a supervisor at Rocky, said, "Don't underestimate yourself on your application." Others have echoed that. Bob, a wonderful volunteer at Rocky gave the same advice, and recommended that I might want to get an EMT (emergency medical technician) certification in order to get a job in interpretation. Any advanced or related training you might get could be helpful and catch the eye of a hiring official.

A hiring official is the person who screens the many certified applicants as determined by the Human Resources Office and makes the final decision in hiring people. Depending on the park, it might be the Chief of Interpretation, an Educational Supervisor, or a GS-9 supervisor or district supervisor.

It seems to me that, unless you are a student intern or a VIP (Volunteer In Parks), having a Bachelor's degree is helpful.

I am not aware of any rangers without that degree. I have known rangers with a variety of college backgrounds—science, history, drama, education, and in my case education with language arts teaching. Many seasonals have teaching degrees.

TRAINING

After you have gotten the job, training will come in many ways—books and materials that are sometimes sent to you ahead of your starting date; usually two weeks of intensive on-the-job training where you read, learn the SOPS (standard operating procedures), shadow other rangers, and perhaps learn about the area where you will be working.

At the Abraham Lincoln Home, my first day was spent visiting other historical sites and city visitor centers. This helps considerably when you are working at a park's visitor center as visitors will often ask about other places where they can go, where housing may be, directions, and other out-of-park questions. You are viewed as a semi-expert in the local area simply because you are working in a "visitor center"—even though it is a park service visitor center, not a city visitor center. My experience is that the parks do not allow you to recommend a specific restaurant or hotel for visitors, even though you may have your favorites. I often ask, "What type of food do you like, and what do you want to spend?" Usually, then, you can give them choices. All parks where I have worked have many materials behind the desk which will help you guide visitors to outside the park businesses and areas. Many cities or the Chambers of Commerce will supply the park with information. Atlases, phone books, and other staff may help.

As you have gathered by now, you are not assigned to a park; rather you apply to a park. As a seasonal, you are not transferred from one park to another. You have control of where you are going, by applying and being accepted where you want to go.

Especially if you have not had a National Park Service position as yet, apply to as many as you can. In one year, I probably applied for twenty-five different positions. One year I had two offers—one at Mt. Rushmore, the other at the Abraham Lincoln Home. Apply at some obscure sites, in order to get started in the National Park Service profession. You may or may not hear from the parks where you apply.

You will be rated up to 100 points based on your experience, education, and background. If you are a veteran, you could be awarded 5 to 10 points additional. For example, if you score 95 on your application, and are a veteran, your score could be 105. Often the park where you applied will send you results of your score and indicate that your application has been sent to the hiring official. Others will not.

Do not be in a hurry to get an answer. Several hiring officials have told me that they appreciate a phone call or an email from an applicant. If you wish, call the park, talk to someone in the human resources office, and ask who the hiring official is.

Call (which I recommend over email) the hiring official who will probably be your boss, and indicate your sincere interest in the position, get time-lines for hiring from them, and ask them if they have any questions of you. I have found all of them receptive to my calls, and later they have told me that they can then put a voice with the application.

How far do you want to go in order to work, and can you travel? Do you have a spouse and/or a pet to take with you? Some parks will not allow either; others will. Working seasonally means that you may not work more than 1039 hours in a park service unit. My shortest season was three months while my longest season was very close to the 1039 hours.

It has always been interesting to me that you can work, in a year's time, (September 1 to August 31), 1039 hours in one park and another 1039 hours in a different park; but you cannot have both seasons in one park—same duty location and successor position as per Office of Personnel Management. I have been told that this prevents the agency from paying most benefits.

You will accrue sick leave and some annual leave, four hours of annual leave per pay period—a two week period or 80 hours of work, and when you have been a seasonal for three total years, you earn six hours of annual leave per pay period. You earn four hours of sick leave per pay period.

Sometimes you can be hired as an intermittent, meaning that the park can determine how many hours you will work in a pay period. Your work will be determined by others' illnesses, their annual leave, or special events.

HOUSING

A CHALLENGE

Finding housing for your seasonal job, is sometimes as big a challenge as getting the job.

Some parks will provide housing, with the rent coming out of your paycheck; other, smaller parks, do not have housing, and you must find it. Rental fees for park housing vary depending on where you are living, having risen in the past few years, matching the local rentals.

If you have a spouse and a pet, the hunt for housing is more difficult. The length of the assignment also can affect your chances. Some renters do not want to rent for a short period of time, and they either don't want a dog, or they will charge you a pet deposit which might be as much as $500, which will be used for any damage. In one apartment, they had to have the carpet cleaned, a $75 cost, after we left—or so they said—which they said was a local requirement.

So, your search can take time. Local newspapers, local realtors, and web sites like *www.craigslist.com* and *www.apartments.com* can help if you have gotten a job in a larger city area.

If you are lucky enough to have park housing, you will find it in many forms—very rustic, less rustic, and rustic.

At Rocky Mountain National Park, I shared a one-bedroom apartment, followed the second season by a wonderfully rustic cabin inside the park.

John was my young roommate the first year, treating me with much respect. We were both hired as park rangers at the entrance stations. It was a basic apartment with a kitchen/eating area; bath, and one bedroom. Furniture, as it is, is furnished, as are some plates and dishes. Not wanting to rough it too much, I subscribed to cable tv. We shared the expense of a telephone, but the rest of the utilities were included in the rent. Several other park apartments were either connected or close by, so you could sometimes hear other people, especially Rob who lived next door and loved to party.

The second summer season, when we did not yet have a dog, my wife accompanied me, and we enjoyed a one-bedroom cabin in the park. It was rustic, but beautifully located with a large living room, antiquated bathroom, small kitchen, and bedroom. The living area had very large windows on three sides, allowing us to view the deer, elk, coyotes, birds and scenery. In both seasons, I walked or rode my bike to work.

My wife really enjoyed that summer, seeing the variety of wildlife. She was, and still is immensely supportive of me, and we enjoyed friends and relatives visiting.

This particular cabin which we lived in during the summer of '95 has since been remodeled, according to the historical standards of the park.

While attending an Elderhostel in San Diego, I received word of my acceptance at John Muir National Historic Site in Martinez, CA. We flew to San Francisco, drove to Martinez, and began an area search for an apartment for us and our 20 lb well-behaved dog. It was Labor Day weekend, so many rental apartment offices were closed.

We continued to search and finally found, but only for myself—no dogs allowed—the Lotus Apartments, about two blocks from the site. The rent for the unfurnished one-bedroom was $800 per month.

You can be creative in finding or taking furniture. The inflatable queen sized bed worked for sleeping; cabinets in the hallway worked as a dresser; a card table and chairs worked for the kitchen; and Cheryl, a part-time ranger at John Muir NHS, sold me an old couch which her husband helped me carry to the second floor apartment. At the end of the season, I gave it to my boss. A lawn chair and a computer table completed the furniture. Later, my boss at Point Reyes would call me a "dumpster dipster" as we would find useful furniture in the apartment complex dumpsters. After finding a plant in the dumpster—a nice plant about two feet high—and watering it for a few weeks, our daughter visited, and noted that it was a plastic plant. We thought it had been growing at bit!

The park ranger job at John Muir was for six months, so it was difficult to be without my wife and our dog. She did fly out, dog included, for a three-week stay at Christmas. My two daughters also made the trip for a few days each.

Walgreens, Safeway, and other stores were close, so I often would not drive for a week at a time. Bicycling, an addiction of mine, was also good in the area. The site was only two blocks away.

In Springfield, IL, where I worked at the Abraham Lincoln Home National Historic Site, it was necessary to search for an apartment which would include places for me, my wife, and our dog. Sometimes, as in this case, a landlord will contact the park indicating he/she had a place available. This landlord had a furnished upstairs apartment, including the utilities, and off-street parking. It had a large living room with an outdoor porch, a large bedroom, adequate kitchen, separate dining room, and a nice bathroom. The rent for this apartment was $600 per month, including utilities, except for the phone line and cable tv. The many trains which passed by, two blocks away, were the only downside. Being so close to the site was wonderful. Having an hour for lunch allowed me to go home. Having grown up in Illinois, we had many relatives in the area and got to see many of them, many of them taking my guided tour.

Since we moved to Estes Park, CO, next to Rocky Mountain National Park, we have built a home, so my housing needs here have been solved since 1995.

At Redwood National and State Parks in Northern California, I spent two winter seasons—the first renting a three-bedroom home in Crescent City, unfurnished; the second season in park housing, without my wife.

Again we used the card table and chairs; a used furniture store provided the $50.00 couch, and we rented a bed for the stay—three months in length. The second season, my wife decided not to go with me, and I had a wonderful three bedroom park house.

It was filthy when I arrived a few days early, so I spent those days cleaning floors, windows, and dishes. All utilities were furnished, and I now had a cell phone, so all I needed was my tv hookup!

This site was absolutely beautiful, and I did not share it with anyone. Looking out the back windows to see the massive redwoods each morning was an inspirational way to start the day. Since the house was near a busy highway, it was nice, also, to have a two-car garage including some weight-lifting equipment. I recommend that you use park housing which helps immerse you in the particular park. My wife came out the last week to see the place, and to help me drive back to Colorado in our pick-up truck. A pick-up can be a great vehicle for working at and moving to various parks.

Perhaps the most demanding place to find housing was when I worked at Point Reyes National Seashore. Using *www.craigslist.com*, I was finally able to find a wife and dog-friendly apartment in Petaluma, California, about a 45 minute drive to the park—a beautiful drive through farmland, hills, trees, and along streams. The second floor apartment had a large living room, a large center room which we used for a bedroom, and a kitchen/dining area and a bath. Utilities were included, except for phone and tv. Incidentally, I have found that the cheap tv antennaes do not work well even though we were close to San Francisco.

The apartment was two blocks from downtown and a square block park, so we enjoyed the walks. A wonderful boss, John, picked me up two or three days a week, saving considerable on auto costs. As in most cases of private housing, be prepared to put down the first month's rent, sometimes the last month, and a deposit. We paid $875 per month, not including utilities. You can usually figure that about one-half of your salary will go for rent and other expenses.

I had only worked three days at the San Francisco Maritime National Historical Park when a family emergency necessitated my returning home. Indeed, finding housing in San Francisco was a challenge! My wife decided not to go for the four-month season. Sometimes, as in the case of John Muir, Redwoods, Point Reyes and Abraham Lincoln, I flew to the area to arrange housing ahead of time. This time I decided to do it by phone and internet. It was not an easy task.

For the first week, I lived in a hotel in the Tenderloin District of San Francisco, interesting to say the least. The hotel had no kitchen facilities and shared showers and bathrooms were down the hall. Working for the park service demands flexibility and tolerance.

22

I was about to pay a $900 monthly down-payment in a closer area when the news came about the family emergency.

I probably spent ten to fifteen hours trying to find housing there. My boss, Kathy, had tried valiantly to find housing for me and another new park guide. Housing costs are extremely high in the San Francisco area. One former seasonal guide spent her entire season, living out of her pickup truck while working in San Francisco.

I do recommend that you go to the site ahead of time, if time and finances allow, to arrange your housing. You can visit the places that might be available, do all of the necessary paperwork, visit the park unit where you will work—in general get the "lay of the land."

I have found searching for housing to be challenging, interesting, and certainly time-consuming.

AND NOW
FOR THE GOOD STUFF!

1994—ROCKY MOUNTAIN NATIONAL PARK

THE ENTRANCE STATION

Imagine how the early Native Americans or early explorers must have viewed this Rocky Mountain area as they came westward. In our case in the 1960's, we traveled westward from Northern Illinois after being referred to the area by friends. As Major Long observed in the 1820's, first were clouds on the horizon, maybe as far east as a hundred miles. But, as we drove closer, it was obvious that these were the mountains, getting ever bigger—snow-capped, rugged, beautiful. And, for many years after, our family trekked westward to enjoy this area, especially Rocky Mountain National Park.

As the years passed, we experienced more of the park—its backcountry area, trails, and even climbing Longs Peak one summer.

In my opinion, its beauty is unsurpassed and somewhat difficult to describe. After living here since 1995, it becomes apparent that there are ever-changing aspects: winds, snow, clouds, shadows, lights, weather, scenery, animals, birds, and people. So many better authors have better described these details in their publications.

So many who live here now, migrated from other parts of the country because of the short-lived beauty they experienced while vacationing here. Each has his own story about what this area has brought to them. In our case, we continue to experience the daily beauty of this area.

If you get the chance sometime, take a "whiff" of this natural, cultural, and historical area. You won't regret it.

My first year working for the National Park Service was as a park ranger at a very busy entrance station, a worthwhile experience, one I won't soon forget.

I had taken an early retirement from teaching in Illinois in 1993, and as a family, had been visiting the Estes Park area and Rocky Mountain National Park for about twenty-five years. In the summers of 1985, '86, and '87, I had worked in downtown Estes Park as a retail clerk and assistant store manager. The town of Estes Park adjoins Rocky Mountain National Park.

After being accepted, we went through a pretty intensive two-week training in order to get ready for the coming summer season. Heidi was my immediate boss at the entrance station, and others working there were Todd, Tracey, Michelle, and Ann.

The kiosk—and there were two at that entrance station at that time—was a very small building, maybe four feet wide and ten or twelve feet long with a door, windows that opened on both sides, and stationary windows facing the incoming and outgoing traffic.

The beauty surrounding this entrance was breath-taking—wildlife, flowers, some of the park's highest peaks visible, and plentiful sunshine.

The work is intense, some days more than others, as you are constantly taking in money—five dollars at that time for a seven-day pass for a vehicle, checking and selling seasonal, national and issuing Golden Age passes, answering questions, and having some fun with other workers. It can certainly be hot in the kiosks with fumes from vehicles getting to you, and sometimes having people on both sides of you, wanting information or having an emergency, and the other side waiting for you to sell them a pass. Since you may be the only ranger many visitors see, often they will want to talk, tell you about their last visit, or chit-chat. That, of course, only slows the line of cars behind them, especially on a very busy Saturday or Sunday in the park. It is a challenging position.

We had several supervisors from the park provide our training. Not one of them was the superintendent. Sometimes, I would give quizzes to the staff who would be going into the park for work. One day, this man arrived, in uniform, and I asked if he wanted to take the daily quiz. He said sure, so I asked him, "How many horseshoes are there in Horseshoe Park?" He did not know. I asked what his position was. He said he was the superintendent. Do you remember those situations where you would like to evaporate? This was one of them. However, he was very kind and gracious and drove off. At least I had gotten to meet him!!

One day a motorcyclist pulling up, handing me a wet crumpled up twenty-dollar bill. It was disgusting. After giving him the change, another employee said he had seen the cyclist taking the bill from the front inside of his pants—near the crotch! I wanted to puke, but there was another smiling visitor waiting! At that time, we did not have Purell. My hands were thoroughly washed at the next break.

It is, of course, illegal to drink and drive, but one day a car load of young people pulled up, and there was a beer between the driver's legs. DUH!! Fortunately, Supervisor Mary, a law enforcement ranger, was on site. I radio her from the kiosk, telling the driver to wait a minute. Mary came out, pulled him over, and made him open them and pour them out. Obviously, he was not happy with me.

We were told that if we were working alone, and traffic backed up so far down the hill that we could not see the end of cars, we could step out and wave everyone through—without them paying. One day, the other ranger was at lunch, and the backup happened. I stepped out and waved thirty-four cars through. The policy was changed that week. People would have to wait.

Having an emergency vehicle come through posed some interesting situations. It might be a law enforcement ranger responding to an emergency, a fire engine, or an ambulance.

The plan was to clear a lane for them to quickly pass through. If you have two lanes with about twenty cars in each, it takes a bit of traffic maneuvering to get a lane cleared, or they can take the out-bound lane, if you can get the out-bound traffic stopped. Usually there was a five or more minute warning from dispatch or the emergency unit. So, this involved going along a lane of cars, having them get to the right, and remaining static as the emergency unit went through. Visitors and park staff were wonderfully cooperative.

One of my frustrating experiences was not to have the shift report come out right at the end of the shift. Obviously, the money you took in had to match the passes you had sold. We were told if you were off more than fifty dollars in a season, you would be fired. Fortunately, wonderful Heidi, the station supervisor, could usually spot the mistake.

One day, many visitors were wishing me a happy birthday!! My birthday is in January; this was mid-August! After people in about 12 cars had wished me a happy birthday, I asked why they thought it was my birthday. They said the other entrance kiosk had a sign on it!! Good old (actually young) Tracey. She had posted a sign in the incoming traffic window. She had the biggest grin when I confronted her. Not to be out-done, I decided to put up a sign on my window indicating that Tracey was getting married the next day!! She caught on quickly after a few visitors congratulated her. We needed a bit of humor to keep our sanity.

We reasoned that Chief Ranger Joe would not have appreciated this, so the signs were removed.

Every two weeks or so, we would get the chance to work at Aspenglen Campground for a day. That was a nice break, and getting to know and getting to help visitors settle in and getting to know the campground hosts was rewarding.

I even had the chance to patrol on a bicycle! One morning, a couple of dogs were loose. One promptly bit the back of my left leg. It was a small wound, but one I needed to report back at the office. Gary, a supervisor, was there, and he called dispatch and soon the campground host, an EMT, arrived as well as Patty, a law enforcement ranger. The EMT gave me a full assessment, wanted to know if I needed an ambulance. I indicated, "no." Patty determined that the dog, a German Shepard, had its current shots. But, it was also determined that I should go to the ER to be examined by a doctor. He gave me a tetanus shot, cleaned the wound, and told me that he had heard that a dog's mouth is probably cleaner than a human's! I still have a small scar there, a reminder of that day's adventures.

Another nice diversion from the entrance station work, was the chance to get to "rove"—that is basically take a hike on one of the trails for a full day.

The idea was for us to answer questions from visitors, check to see if the trail was clear and safe, and have a respite from the entrance station work. It was another great way to get to know the park, allowing us to impart that knowledge to incoming visitors. The beauty and diversity of the trails always brought about a feeling of awe.

In mid-September, near the end of my season, the chief ranger not only brought us all fudge bars, but also said to me, "You are still smiling at the end of the season."

Truly, I had enjoyed my first experience in the National Park Service.

I would recommend anyone work at an entrance station if that is what it takes to get into the service. It will give you some great experience, and you will get to know park staff, and the park as well. As we were often told, you might be the only ranger visitors see, and it is so important to give a positive contribution. As you apply, instead of checking for a park ranger's job, look at listings, "Visitor Use Assistant."

Sometimes you will get an in-depth question about your park or the park system. Kevin wrote me a nice note which I received on December 27, 1994. "Thank you for all the information that you sent me. It was a pleasure talking to you about National Parks. My goal is to get my feet wet by getting started in local and state parks before moving on. Again, you have been a great help."

1995—ROCKY MOUNTAIN NATIONAL PARK

EMT DUTY

During the spring months of 1995, I took the basic Emergency Medical Technician training at KSB Hospital in Dixon, IL, successfully passing the course by the end of May, shortly before starting my second season at Rocky as an interpretative ranger/EMT. My ten hour day, four days a week was three days at the Alpine Visitor Center, 11,760 feet above sea level, an area where medical incidents number about 100 per season. Most of the incidents are connected with high altitude problems, including asthma, cardiac problems, dizziness, nausea, and other assorted problems.

If needed, the closest ambulance at Estes Park would take forty-five minutes before arriving on scene.

AVC (Alpine Visitor Center) sits at the crest of a significant drop-off, massive windows allowing visitors to sense the scenery below, including permanent snow fields, sometimes with elk or deer present. The views are unimaginable—various rock formations formed by ancient glaciers, trickling water cascading downward, elk so far away looking like ants as they graze unaware of the many people observing them from the steep hill above. Because of the strong winds and heavy snow in the winter, AVC is only open during summer months.

I remember vividly a visitor coming in early in the season indicating that a bus had gone off the road about five miles east of the center. I asked whether it had turned over, were there any injuries, etc. The visitor knew that the bus had gone off the road, that it was still upright, but was not sure if there were any injuries. I radioed our dispatch to determine if I should respond as I was the only EMT on duty that day at the AVC. Since most of the law enforcement rangers were in training that day, and the closest was near our headquarters about forty-five minutes away, they said for me to respond. Earlier, Doug, the district law-enforcement ranger, said that we could only drive ten miles over the speed limit responding to emergencies, using the wig-wag lights on front of the vehicle.

I arrived fifteen to twenty minutes later at the bus, which had gone off the road on the right side. Fortunately, where it had gone off was about one-hundred yards after a drop-off. The driver was very embarrassed, saying he had been driving for years, but had encountered a fog and simply drove off the road.

I quickly boarded the bus to determine if there were any injuries. Besides the driver, only one other person spoke English, all being from Japan. I asked if everyone was all right, and proceeded to go down the aisle slowly, visually checking each person. All appeared OK.

Now what? I had difficulty reaching ROMO, our dispatch, with my hand-held radio, so had to go back to the car radio. They said they would dispatch a law enforcement ranger and a tow truck, both of which would take about forty-five minutes. In the meantime, maintenance worker, Bob, had arrived, and because of heavy traffic and low visibility, we slowed the traffic from each direction. I checked two more times with the passengers to be sure no one was injured or suffering the effects of stress and altitude. Soon law enforcement ranger, Curt, arrived, and I was released to return to AVC.

We never knew when someone would suddenly become ill. Since we did a couple of programs each day, a medical might occur in the middle of a program. The other ranger or the book store clerk would yell, "We have a medical." We would say, "Sorry, but this program is over, due to a medical emergency." Then we would respond to what was occurring. Since the Trail Ridge Store was about 30 yards away, we would often respond to the store for someone who had fainted, felt dizzy, or just "didn't feel all right." An employee would alert us to the medical. Any age can be affected by high altitude problems.

Because we worked three 10-hour days, we were able to work one day in the lower elevations for 10 hours, making our 40 hour week. I had the opportunity to do an evening program at the small Aspenglen Campground where about 50 to 75 people would show up after I did a "tour" of the campground, informing them of my program, called "The Web of Life." It was a general program about animals and plants of the park and how they were interrelated. I did an exercise where I spread string among about 10 visitors who had signs hanging on them—e. g. water to coyote; fire to forest, etc. It was the concluding part of the forty-five minute presentation, after the slide portion of the program.

I liked the intimacy of that amphitheatre, being so close to the visitors with the trees and stream nearby and the mountains towering a half-mile away. One evening a great horned owl completely overshadowed and stopped my program, by landing above the stage and staring at the audience.

Having the opportunity to work with Bob, a retired veterinarian and Rocky VIP/EMT, was always rewarding. We often worked as a team with a patient at Alpine Visitor Center, receiving a wonderful letter from Mr. and Mrs. Crews of Indiana who wrote, "We need to give our special thanks for the tremendous and sensitive support that you gave to our son, Will, at your first aid station this summer. You might recall our family rushing into your station at the Alpine Visitor Center on July 27 with Will in our arms. He had fallen while climbing ("jumping," he corrects us) on rocks at the top of the trail. Will had a serious gash on his chin and a sore arm. Not only did the two of you console our frightened five-year-old, but you bandaged his chin, put a splint on his arm and patiently checked for other possible injuries. We thank you for your terrific service, and for your true sensitivity and care." This is what the Service is all about.

This being my first summer as an EMT at the AVC, my supervisor, Carol, wanted to surprise each of us with a medical scenario. So, on my day, she came to the counter, indicating (as a patient) that she had fallen at the Trail Ridge Store, and needed help. So I accompanied her to the med room, began taking vitals, putting on a c-collar, and was about to administer oxygen when a real patient came in—suffering high altitude sickness. Carol assisted, then actually took over, to help this patient who ultimately had to be transported to the local hospital. In the meantime, another patient came in, less severe, but needed oxygen and needed to be put in a reclining position; remember only one hospital bed. High above the first patient was one of the cots we could use with multiple patients. The shelf holding the cots was about seven feet above the first patient. As I reached for the cot, my foot slipped slightly, and the cot came tumbling down, just missing the first patient!

1996—ROCKY MOUNTAIN NATIONAL PARK

MEDICINE AT HIGH ALTITUDE

Todd, a wonderfully, effusive young EMT/ranger, seemed to attract problems at AVC. He found a dead body there; performed CPR on an elderly lady who later died; he almost always had the most serious medicals that occurred at AVC. He handled all of them with professionalism.

One day when he was passing through on his day off, we got the call that a car had gone off the road about three to four miles west of AVC. Dispatch said for us to respond because the only law enforcement ranger available was on back-country patrol on the west side of the park. Todd said he would respond with me. We piled in the jeep, took off, wig-wags going, arriving on the scene. A sleepy driver had gone off the road and down the hill slightly. He was outside the vehicle as were his two boys and wife. It was obvious he was in considerable pain. Fortunately, a doctor was on scene as well. All of this was in a pretty narrow part of the road, and we had our vehicle on the downhill lane, blocking west-bound traffic. A wonderful volunteer came along and helped direct traffic while we called for a west-side ambulance. The back-country ranger was responding to his car—each taking about 45 minutes to get there.

Todd and I attempted to get the man on a backboard, but with his intense pain, we decided to wait until the ambulance personnel arrived. We continued to monitor vitals and make him as comfortable as possible, also checking his two sons. Both of them seemed all right, later finding out that one had a perforated stomach. In the meantime, traffic was backed up each way for a few miles, but the volunteer kept one-way traffic going as best he could. Finally, the ambulance arrived. We were able to get the man on the backboard, transported to the local hospital and later air-lifted to a Steamboat Springs hospital. He had sustained multiple injuries, including a broken pelvis. I later got to talk to him in Longmont, CO while he was making a long recovery. The park received a nice letter, especially praising Todd for his work on his day off.

Another day, Hanna and I were working at the AVC. I had gone to do the "Tundra Walk," a 1 ½ hour walk/talk about three or four miles east of the AVC at the semi-flat area called "Ice-berg Pass." After the program, arriving back at the AVC, Hanna was working with a patient outside the center.

The patient was sitting on the curb. Hanna yelled, "Can you handle this one? There is another one already in the medical room." I said sure and began the assessment. The elderly lady was having severe chest pain, clutching her chest. Someone said, give her Nitro! I said that I could not administer any drugs.

But another visitor, along with a pretty large crowd who had gathered, insisted that she take some nitro. One man in particular insisted, and I asked if he were a doctor, and he said yes. So, I said if you want to give it to her, go ahead. The medication soon took effect; meantime Hanna had called for an ambulance for the altitude sickness case inside. I had gotten a visitor to get a wheelchair for my patient and wheeled her inside to the medical room where Hanna's patient was, plus another one who was not feeling well. The ambulance arrived and transported the first patient; mine had recovered enough to go downhill with her family, and the third one had taken enough oxygen to move on.

Now, let me describe that medical room. Its door was immediately off of the lobby of the AVC, had no windows, often became hot, housed one hospital bed and two cots which we could put up for additional patients. When you got two or three patients in the room plus a couple of EMT's, it became just a bit crowded and gamey.

Sometimes, only the book store clerk would be available to answer questions and sell items for the 5,000 visitors who might visit the AVC during a summer day. Those clerks are fantastic!

Some very nice visitors took the time to fill out a "Visitor Comment Form" which then goes to the Superintendent who reviews it and sends it down the chain of command to our supervisor. It is usually unexpected and very much appreciated. On July 12, 1996, a visitor from CO wrote, "We had the wonderful experience of spending two hours with Dick Boyer on his 'Signs of Life' walk/talk. Dick was informative, enthusiastic, and very friendly. He is the *model* of what a N.P.S. naturalist should be and do. Please pass our praise on to him."

On July 16, 1996, some nice folks from Dallas wrote, "Ranger Dick Boyer's 1 ½—2 hr. talk on the tundra was outstanding! He did a terrific job. We all learned a lot. Also, we love Ranger talks—please keep as many as possible." One of their children wrote, "Ranger Dick was very friendly, and he answered all questions with thorough answers. He didn't think any of them were stupid."

We often say to visitors, don't think any of your questions are stupid. Some of them are interesting, but never stupid.

July, 1996, was a good month for me as another visitor from NY wrote, "You have no reason to remember me, especially because I did not introduce myself to you, but I was a member of your Tundra session. When you sat down at the end of our session you appeared completely relaxed and in harmony with nature. I took your photo with the intent of sending it to you and here it is. I have visited most of America's National Parks and I have never found a more enthusiastic and engaging group of naturalists. Kathleen, who lead a photo session that I attended, and you are both credits to RMNP!"

1997—ROCKY MOUNTAIN NATIONAL PARK

A PRINCESS PASSES OUT!

One day at the AVC, having just gone to lunch in one of the back apartments, Jan, the store clerk, the only other person on duty, radioed that a person had passed out just inside the front entrance to the center. Leaving my lunch, not an unusual occurrence, hurrying to the lobby area, I found a young lady, perhaps in her twenties, lying on the floor, with a young man and several others around her. I introduced myself as she was becoming conscious, insisting on a full assessment and getting her on oxygen. She agreed as did her fiance, and we got her into the med room. After vitals and administration of oxygen, she was responding well. But, unfortunately, her fiance was not! He was sobbing, moving about the room; I thought I was going to have two patients at once! Trying to calm him down, I finally got him to relax as she continued to bounce back. About twenty minutes into the oxygen therapy, she was about to be dismissed.

I went out of the med room, and was explaining to her entourage, about five or six people, that she was a bit dehydrated, and probably suffering from a light case of altitude sickness. They all bowed profusely, and indicated that the country of Malaysia was extremely thankful!! I was taken aback, to say the least.

As I released her, the bows continued and they all left. I am not sure who she was, but apparently someone of significance.

About a year later, there was a contact at Camp Cheley, a private youth camp south of Estes Park, asking for me. I tried without success to get back to them, but it was one of those experiences which proves to me that many, many good people exist, and are grateful for help.

One afternoon, an older gentleman became ill in the Trail Ridge Store next door. He was obviously having altitude sickness, a high heart rate, and was nauseated. Our procedure was to go there with a wheelchair, make a quick assessment, and transport them back to the med room for further treatment. Just as we got into the med room, he vomited all over the front of himself and onto my shoes. He and his wife were extremely embarrassed, not being a big deal for me as this often happens. So, I indicated "no problem," determined that he was stabilizing and getting better on the administered oxygen. He had extra clothes in his car so his family cleaned him up, and after a bit more oxygen and a final assessment of his vitals, he left after expressing much gratitude.

When you are dealing with the physical, stressful mental aspects of people, it can be quite frightening to them.

Sometimes visitors would actually collapse in the parking lot, and that is where you would go to treat them—assessing, taking vitals, usually getting them on oxygen, hoping for a quick recovery.

High altitude can affect any age group and any body type. Patients might collapse in Trail Ridge Store, or on the steep Alpine Ridge Trail. Usually a relative, friend, or another visitor would come in, obviously a bit panicked, and indicate that someone was having trouble. The procedure: get the oxygen, the wheelchair, a backboard, and take off for the incident. It was always an adrenalin rush as you started out, not knowing what you might be facing. If there were two EMT's, one assumed the role of the lead, directing the other on what to do, getting the history, age, address, medications, and filling out the medical "run" sheet.

Sue and I were working one afternoon as a visitor came in yelling that a man was coming with a child who was not breathing. Talk about an adrenalin rush! We both went outside to intercept the man. Fortunately, the child, less than one year old, was again breathing, getting her color back. Dealing with a small child can be challenging, as they are not sure what is happening, and the parent can also be very distraught—which is only natural—and the child is in constant movement! With the father's help, the child reacted quickly and effectively with the oxygen.

We monitored the child closely for several minutes, but even before releasing the patient, we highly recommended that the child go to the hospital on the way out of the park, just to be sure. We gave the child a small stuffed bear, those being provided by a wonderful retired telephone workers group. Stuffed bears can help sooth the injured souls.

Getting to do some interpretative programs was a nice diversion from dealing with medicals and answering questions at the information desk.

At least once a week, I had the opportunity to do a "Tundra Nature Walk." It was advertised in the park newspaper, but there was no sign-up, so we never knew how many visitors would show up. The program was at 10:00 a.m. We would gather at the flagpole outside AVC; then a short introduction was given about the program, and we would carpool to Iceberg Pass, about three or four miles east.

The program was so enjoyable. Parking was available and then it was a litany of rules on the tundra—stay on rocks where possible, don't walk single file, and, of course, don't pick any flowers or take anything.

My talk included getting people down on all fours to smell the Forget-me-Nots—a pungent citrus smell; experiencing the boundary layer; finding the marmot den; moving to the other side of the road to do a "framing" activity where the group was broken into family units, and each was to put a square foot frame down on the ground and then to list everything in the frame—having only five minutes to do so. Many would forget what was above the ground. Other features of the tundra included the small limber pines, the solifluction terraces, and often glimpses of elk. Of course, the unlimited scenery could be seen in all directions.

Another program done at the center was "Alpine Aspects," a thirty minute program about geology, plants, and animals of the tundra. Having some interesting fellow rangers there, made it more challenging. Often, behind the crowd, a puppet would appear with its mouth moving, or perhaps dancing, or going up and down or back and forth. I always did likewise to them when I had the chance. With the stress at the center, we needed some comic relief!

We never knew what we might be asked to do. One day, a middle-aged couple came in to say they had dropped their movie camera down the slope behind the center. A young law enforcement ranger, David, was there, but did not want to scramble down the rather steep hill to get the camera. So, I decided to descend.

About one-hundred yards down the steep area was the broken camera—maybe three pieces, some of it still missing. Not finding the remaining parts, I scrambled and huffed up the hill. To my amazement, after giving the parts to the couple, they said nothing, and seemed to be angry at me, leaving quickly.

This was the year that several of the Trail Ridge store employees would get sick—usually at least one a day. We quickly found out that some of them were playing sick to get out of work, lying in our hospital bed, taking oxygen, resting and getting paid for it. Needless to say the practice soon came to a halt.

A quick assessment was made when one came in, and usually they were given a ten-minute rest, re-assessed, and sent back to work!

Taking anything from a national park unit is forbidden, including elk antlers. But a visitor pointed out that about one mile back on Old Fall River Road, there was a pick-up that had stopped, and a man was collecting antlers. About that time a law enforcement officer, in uniform but off-duty, came in with his family. We watched from the back of AVC as the antler collecting continued. The LE ranger asked if I would take him down Old Fall River Road—a one-way up road. He contacted dispatch to let them know what he was doing. We put the wig-wags on while swerving around up-coming traffic. We stopped a couple hundred yards uphill from the collector. In the mean-time, another LE ranger had come up from below and was approaching.

Both descended on the collector, much to his surprise. He was cited for taking a natural resource from the park, and the antlers were confiscated.

Another interesting activity that occurred at AVC was when people locked their ignition keys in their vehicle. I became proficient in opening vehicles with the "slim-jim," a flat, metal device that would get down into the door between the window and the frame. I had a 100% success rate. Those who did lock their keys up were always embarrassed, but always happy when I could get in, sometimes within a few seconds.

One visitor said that his brand new truck was supposed to be tamper proof!

Often as rangers we are asked to have our pictures taken with visitors.

I have had mine taken with little people, big people, "Flat Stanley" (a writing program for school children). Perhaps the most interesting was with a pink flamingo from Kansas. The lady who talked me into this was secretary in the Speech Communication Department at Washburn University in Topeka, KS. She wrote on June 5, 1997, "Please find enclosed a photo taken of you on Friday, May 30, 1997, with our famous flamingo, Pinky Lee. If I remember correctly you were hoping that she would be Brooke Shields! Thank you for agreeing to pose for the picture . . . I have put a copy of your picture and the Ranger badge that you gave Pinky Lee into our scrapbook . . . Your famous partner is now off to Obbola, Sweden and her partner is off to the Czech Republic. We are hoping that someday one of our famous pair will show up on Leno, Letterman or the Rosie O'Donnell Shows."

Often we hear from visitors from other countries. A gentleman from the UK wrote, "My wife and I have recently returned from a two-week holiday in Estes Park. We spent most days in your glorious park and we write simply to thank you for making we visitors so welcome. We were particularly impressed by the quality and dedication of your rangers.

We should particularly like to name Dick Boyer, Don and Chase as being outstanding in their knowledge, presentation, courtesy and friendliness. We learned a great deal from them, not least about American warmth and generosity of spirit."

1998—ROCKY MOUNTAIN NATIONAL PARK

DESCENDING TO LOWER

ELEVATIONS

After three stressful years as an EMT at AVC, I asked for a re-assignment as a five-day park ranger interpreter in the lower elevations. Fortunately, I was granted that assignment for the summer of 1998.

Working in the lower elevations allowed me to work at the Moraine Park Museum, Beaver Meadows Visitor Center, and Sheep Lakes Information Station. In addition, I did several programs, including an evening program at Aspenglen Campground, called "The Web of Life."

Moraine Park Museum is a beautiful museum, situated in Moraine Park, home to a couple of programs: "Moraine Park Nature Walk" in the morning and "Rivers of Ice" in the afternoon.

The morning walk allowed people to accompany me on an hour and half walk which is about a mile in length. Topics included history, geology, flora, and fauna in the montane ecosystem. It was easy to engage people in activities and in appreciation of the scenery. The afternoon program, a shorter one-half hour, was usually held in the upstairs windowed room that overlooks the incredibly vast glaciated meadow.

Would you believe a lady fell asleep while I was doing the program? It was mid-afternoon, so I took a picture I was using in the program, approached her slowly, and touched her arm with the picture, much to the delight of the other visitors. She awoke suddenly, apologized profusely, and was alert the rest of the program.

Sometimes there would be as many as forty-five attending; other times only two. On one walk, only an older couple, both a bit infirmed with limps and canes, made the trip with me, all of us enjoying the experience.

Vividly I remember a geologist attending my Rivers of Ice program—mostly about the glaciers and their effects in developing Moraine Park. Fortunately, he did not tell me he was a geologist until after the program!! I would have been a nervous wreck, but he indicated that he thought I did a good job—maybe being kind.

A very nice July 20 letter and picture were received from Amanda who wrote, "Thank you for all your help with my Science Fair project on rocks. I titled it 'America Rocks.' I received a Certificate of Merit from my School Fair and from the Frederick, CO fair. I'm going into fourth grade this fall and will have to do a different science fair project. Thank you for making my 1st project a prize winner."

MEETING RACHEL

It was this year that I met Rachel and her family. Rachel was about seven or eight, and she and her family went on my Hollowell Park beaver walk/talk. She was so interested in every aspect of this magnificent animal.

On July 14, her parents, Paul and Michelle from Cedar Park, TX wrote, "On July 3, 1999, our family attended your morning ranger program on the beavers in Hollowell Park. We are from the Austin, TX area, and we spoke briefly at the end of the program about cycling and things to see around the Hill Country. Our daughters, Rachel (8) and Hannah (4) thoroughly enjoyed the presentation. Rachel was your model for the beaver pelt headwrap and hung on your heels during the walk. I'm hoping these facts will somehow jog your memory, because we have a very special request of your time and expertise."

They wanted me to assist Rachel who was in a gifted program at her school, by being an "expert" contact for beaver information. She was to do an independent study, and chose beavers. I was to furnish any information that she might need. I said I would have to ask my boss LaShelle if that would be all right. LaShelle said that it would be fine.

During the school year, I supplied Rachel with additional materials, answered emails, and got some pictures of her presentation which seemed amazing for such a young child. It was obvious that she was gifted, and had loving and supportive parents. I also purchased a beaver puppet for her before she left. Rachel wrote later and said, "Thank you so much for the beaver puppet. I love it so much. I wish I could see you this summer. I miss you very much! Love, Rachel"

This kind of experience with park visitors is what it is all about!

My evening program was called "Heart of the Highlands," where another ranger called me the "prop" king! Indeed many props were used in the amphitheatre to bring the tundra to the visitors. Carpet patches simulated the rocks in the tundra; pictures of the flowers were used, interspersing them among the "rocks." I became "Dr. Tundralove," a Russian scientist who had 30 years experience in studying the tundra. Through supervisor Judy's help, the park purchased a tape of English/Russian dialects, and playing it back and forth to work, I learned to speak with a Russian accent. Leaving the stage briefly to don a Russian hat, a lab coat, and a cane, I became Dr. Tundralove. My supervisor at the time, Jean, still calls me Dr. Tundralove.

One visitor, identifying himself as a professional actor, said I did an excellent job staying in character with Dr. Tundralove. Anyway, to me, it was fun, being able to have the latitude that most supervisors allow for this type of program. Hopefully, the varied, beautiful, and expansive tundra was made real.

That summer I developed a new evening program, "The Majestic Elk." Each evening program developed, at least for me, takes hours to develop. It, at that time, involved deciding on what slides to use, pulling them from the file, writing a 45 minute script, getting them to mesh, and then developing the theme, goals, and objectives and program outline. Through another ranger's help and her generous offering of her slides, it came together.

Through five different supervisors, I have gotten excellent advice on how to improve. I give the visitors a test to begin with; before that I have put several signs of characteristics of elk around the necks of some audience members. Then about one-third of the way into the program, we build an elk, having each one come up to the stage, as I explain that part of the elk. Seemingly, this mammal, that is so plentiful in Rocky, is brought to life. The program continues with narration and slides with quotes from *Among the Elk* coming as a conclusion. Visitors are so interested in this animal, often seeing them near a campground or perhaps near Trail Ridge Road.

Another program that year was "Rocky After Dark." It was limited to 35 participants, done after dark, starting at 9:00 p.m. around Sprague Lake, using all five senses to get participants to appreciate, not only their ability to function in the dark, but also to appreciate how animals function.

John, from Des Moines, IA wrote, on July 6, "We recently returned from a week-long vacation in Estes Park. We spent a great deal of time in Rocky while we were there and were able to attend and participate in a number of ranger-led programs. Of the programs that we attended we had the privilege of having you as our ranger for three of the programs. You had a great rapport with the younger folks in our group. I would bet that if asked about future careers my seven-year old son, would probably have *park ranger* at the top of his list. He thoroughly enjoyed "Rocky After Dark," "Importance of Being a Beaver," and the wildlife program at Sheep's Lake. Keep up the great and valuable work—I hope to see you again the next time that we are at Rocky." The one and half-hour program moved folks to areas around the lake, gently urging them to use their senses in experiencing this unique nature! We never know what types of influences we might have on someone.

During this time working at Rocky, when off-duty, I was also volunteering as a victim's advocate for the Estes Valley Victim Advocates.

This agency helps victims who have experienced a death in the family; domestic violence; and many other crises which might affect a family.

On August 5, I received a call from a park dispatcher that my services were needed for a family that might have experienced a death of a family member. Usually I was involved when I was not working at the park, but this time I was asked to make an on-duty contact with a family in Estes Park.

Jim, a visitor from New York, had been climbing with his son near Longs Peak and fell. A very difficult search was initiated by the park service to find Jim, hopefully alive, and bring him down. Jim was climbing the Loft Route, an approach to Longs Peak from the saddle between Longs and Mt. Meeker, and was with his 28 year old son, Sam. Weather conditions became very poor, with rain and heavy fog. Both Jim and his son were experienced in mountain travel and had previously summited Longs Peak through the more common Keyhole route.

Jim fell 90 feet because of slick, wet rock. Sam witnessed his dad's fall about noon on the 4th and made his way to his dad, staying with him for more than three hours, protecting him with spare clothing, and calling for help with the aid of a whistle. Because he could not contact anyone, Sam had to leave to find help. He was met by a park search team. The teams worked and continued in fog and darkness, finding Jim deceased because of significant head injuries

Sam, of course, was devastated, having to leave his dad.

I was asked to respond as a park ranger/victim advocate, meeting Sam and his mother, Judy at a rental home, near downtown Estes Park. Earl, another victim advocate, was also there. We were asked to stay with the family, one at a time, until Jim's body was brought down, assisting them in any way possible. Earl stayed the night until 3:00 a.m., and then I showed up to stay. Early that morning, Fran, in charge of the park's dispatch services, showed up to let the family know that Jim was deceased, his body had been found, and that park staff were trying to get his body down. The removal of the body was extremely dangerous in very bad weather—with 22 people, including 14 park personnel in four search teams, so we waited and waited, until the body was finally brought down by helicopter.

We assisted them with food, with information from the park, and by taking Sam back to Longs Peak trailhead to get the family car. It was an honor, yet sad, for me to work with these wonderful people and other relatives who came to wait.

My wife, Dorothy, who is known at several of the sites for making home-made cinnamon roles, made some for the family. Earl and I continued to assist.

The family decided to have the body cremated and have a memorial service in the park. Earl, being a retired minister, was asked to provide the service at the Moraine Park Museum amphitheater. I simply kept visitors out of the area, and then on to Forest Canyon overlook to scatter the ashes. After the service, both of us were invited to a dinner at the Stanley Hotel. The family, especially Judy and Sam, were extremely thankful.

One of the most touching thank-you cards I received came from Sam. He wrote, "You did all the right things, and with much good humor, from sitting alone and alert in the living room through the night, to excusing yourself at the perfect moments. Through it all, you displayed tact like I've seen in very, very few people, and a graciousness that was real and not superficial. You provided a stability, a peace, and a strength that helped support us through that chaotic week, until we were able to collect ourselves again and move forward. With each additional sensitive and careful thing you did and said for us, you reaffirmed my belief that there actually are people in the world who genuinely and consistently care about this world and the people they share it with. Sam"

About three weeks later his mother, Judy, wrote, "It's hard to believe that I've been home for almost three weeks. Needless to say, I cannot let another day slip by without pausing to let you know, once again, that I continue to be oh so grateful for your compassionate service to our family during those overwhelmingly dark days of Aug. 4-15. Your kind, gentle spirit and helpful deeds truly ministered God's comfort, mercy and love to our aching hearts. Thank you, thank you for giving of yourself in such a powerful way."

Both of these genuine people touched me deeply as I worked through this tragedy with them. You never know how you may be asked to assist visitors and how you might affect their experiences—whether sad or happy. The most difficult thing was to remain focused and not to get emotionally involved—sometimes keeping the tears hidden away!

It is probably unlikely that you would be involved in this type of NPS service unless specifically trained to do so.

From a wonderful couple, William and Patricia, of Richmond Texas, came a note on September 14, 1999—along with a $50.00 check made out to RMNP—to support ranger programs. They wrote, "My wife and I spent two lovely weeks in RMNP. I believe that part of that time was made special by ranger programs. We had the opportunity of enjoying (participating in) three programs which were hosted by you. They were a discussion about Elk (I was the body), a nature walk at Moraine Park and a visit to a beaver pond (we did not actually see any beavers!!—unless you count one on the mountain). Your delivery and mastery of the topics made the events spring to life . . . We have visited several of the national and state parks through out the US.

Aside from the natural beauty and recreational activities afforded by the park systems, we have always enjoyed the ranger programs. We wish to thank you and all of the RMNP staff for their dedication and efforts to preserve the park and its inhabitants, thereby allowing us the opportunity of the occasional visit."

Something always emphasized by our supervisors, is that "connection" with the visitor.

My bosses have always allowed me to appear in uniform and with props to talk to my grandchildren's classes, especially in the Columbus, OH area.

After a November, 1999 visit to Violet Elementary, Pickerington, OH, the students developed a couple of beautiful poems and sent them back to me. The first one read,

Moose Cake

By an icy crystal lake
While the moose fight on the prairies
In the cool evening the black shadows form.

Dedicated to Mr. Boyer with our thanks. Mrs. Roesch's Fourth Grade Students.

The Crystalline Mountains

Where the climbers touch the sky
As white snow creates a crystalline blanket,
The sparkling aquamarine waters turn to ice.

Dedicated to Mr. Boyer with our thanks.
Miss Martin's Fourth Grade Students

Both of these meant much to me. All students had signed the laminated poems.

2000—ROCKY MOUNTAIN NATIONAL PARK

THE SHEEP ARE COMING

DOWN

One of the rewarding and interesting aspects of working at Rocky has been the Sheep Lakes area where each summer a ranger is stationed from 8:30 to 4:00 with four volunteers.

We all give information about the bighorn sheep, direct traffic, give out information and generally protect the sheep. The ranger gives two thirty-minute talks a day regarding the bighorn. It is a chance to be outside all day in a beautiful area of the park—Horseshoe Park, and is also a chance to get to know the volunteers and park visitors.

Studying this incredible symbol of Rocky, also the state mammal of Colorado, is enjoyable—its illusiveness, its beauty, its unpredictability. Visitors, rangers and volunteers are intrigued with their ruggedness and beauty. Interesting, too, is when the sheep decide to appear at Sheep Lakes, seeking the many minerals they lick for nourishment.

The Fall River Visitor Center, opened May, 2000, and I had the opportunity to work at the information desk. The center was financed with private funds, and had to be approved by congress as it is outside the park limits.

Wonderful animal displays, and a "Discovery Room" are included downstairs and there is also a chance for children to try on ranger clothes, native American clothes, and early settlers' clothes. Visitors are also intrigued by the displays, the architecture, and the information provided.

2000, 2001 — JOHN MUIR NATIONAL HISTORIC SITE

HOME TO AN ICON

In November, 2000, I got the chance to work my first winter seasonal job at the John Muir National Historic Site, in Martinez, CA, about an hour northeast of San Francisco.

The site includes the home where John Muir lived and wrote most of his articles and books, the orchard grounds, an Adobe, and about two blocks away, the beautiful Mt. Wanda, named after one of his daughters—a place where you can escape the bustle of the area, climbing to a peaceful, beautifully treed and flowered area.

Being used to the large Rocky Mountain National Park, it was somewhat of a shock to see the small site, actually driving past it twice before seeing the NPS sign announcing it. Each NPS unit brings its own uniqueness. This was no exception—the small visitor center/theatre/bookstore; the stately 10,000 square feet Muir home; the variety of vegetation; the striking Sequoia tree that Muir planted; and meandering path through the grounds, ending at the adobe.

Having the chance to interpret the life and works of John Muir was extremely rewarding. The main thrust of the job was to conduct tours of the home for fourth graders who were studying California history and for the general public who came to tour.

So, within a few days after starting, and after observing other staff members doing tours, I had my tour ready, always flexible to changes at the suggestion of a wonderful boss, David. He was, as in the case of so many other supervisors—supportive, pleasant, knowledgeable, and helpful.

Getting to know this outstanding conservationist and preservationist John Muir was not only an in-depth learning experience, but also would lead to direct connections to Rocky and Enos Mills.

Getting to know the house—its story and how it connected to John Muir and especially his "scribble den" as he called it, helped tell the story to visitors. A short film about Muir was encouraged and then a tour of the home and grounds. Many times volunteers would assist in the tours and be in the house to welcome visitors. It was a challenge, yet fun, to squeeze an entire fourth grade class into the "scribble den" explaining where Muir wrote so many books and articles, having them experience this fruitful room, imagining Muir's presence, and his struggles with writing.

Herb, the head of maintenance, had a degree in horticulture, so the grounds for the site were immaculate and historically accurate. He was assisted by a group of Master Gardeners.

One school group, stood close to the sequoia tree and put their arms around it; Herb gently reminded me that that might disturb the tree, causing harm, so it was introduced from a distance.

In making the connection between Muir and Enos Mills, considered the "father" of Rocky Mountain National Park, I found that they had met in San Francisco and kept a friendship through letters and Mills' visits to the Muir home in Martinez. Muir encouraged Mills to get Rocky Mountain National Park established. It appears that the influence on Mills was remarkable. Who better to influence anyone toward establishing more national parks than John Muir. Muir also felt inspired by Mills.

David and the rest of the staff were supportive in a number of ways—allowing me to make some off-site presentations; allowing me to develop some bulletin board displays regarding Muir and one that featured the small staff; allowing me to develop the first Junior Ranger booklet for the site; and supporting me with my first "mobile" which featured several cards hanging from a coat hanger—three rows with nouns, adjective, and verbs about Muir—perhaps about 12 to 15, 4 X 6 note cards—all hanging from the coat hanger. In the attic at the end of a school tour, I had the teachers and students, using the cards, develop sentences regarding Muir. David even presented the mobile as another way to interpret Muir at a Muir conference. This first mobile lead to another one being developed for school children at the Abraham Lincoln Home NHS the following year.

2001—ROCKY MOUNTAIN NATIONAL PARK

"CLARA, THE COYOTE"

Sometimes, as seasonals, we get the chance to help with new seasonal training, taking newbies on a tour of the area—including the Twin Owls area, through town, and along the east edge of the park, along the route seven corridor and to Wild Basin. They are always inquisitive, a bit intimidated, and overwhelmed by all of the materials they are asked to absorb in a short period of time, all of which is necessary for them to do a good job of interpreting.

My season this summer ran from late May to October. Programs included "Longs Peak Impressions," an evening program comparing and contrasting John Muir and Enos Mills and working at two visitor centers: Moraine Park Museum and Fall River Visitor Center.

One new program was given to me: "Tales for Tots and Big People Two," done at the Fall River Visitor Center. Using a large map of the park with two flaps in it, I introduced the children and parents or grandparents to Roddy the Redtail Hawk and Clara the Coyote who made appearances through those flaps. They talked about the various altitudes of the park, rules, and safety, I being the voice behind these two characters. Before the program, several pelts, antlers, and stuffed animals were introduced to the children, and each child was given one to show the audience as either Roddy or Clara would explain the animal. Then I would take all of them outside on the back patio, and each child would have a picture of an animal placed backward on him/her. Parents then would attempt to figure out the animal by asking questions of each child. It was a way to learn about the animals and yet have some fun doing it. Finally, the web of life was conducted where the children had signs around their necks—water, air, sun, hawk, bear, etc. Then a string is held by the child holding water and stretched to anything that depends on water. So, you get a web of life with all of these string attachments, showing relationships among items of nature. Parents had signs around them—condos, fire, pollution, humans, traffic. They come close to the web, and a discussion followed about how these affect the park and nature. Hopefully, they could see relationships and some adverse affects.

2002—LINCOLN HOME NATIONAL HISTORIC SITE

AND ROCKY MOUNTAIN NATIONAL PARK

In January, 2002, I was hired as a park guide at the Lincoln Home National Historic Site in Springfield, IL. The site offers considerable history and information regarding this sixteenth president. Located in downtown Springfield, IL, four large square blocks encompass the site. With the roads closed within the site, visitors can pick up their free tickets for the tour at the visitor center, located one block from Lincoln's home. Other structures abound, many dating back to Lincoln's seventeen years spent there. Two small museums allow visitors to absorb information about the structures of homes there, and the other featuring the Lincolns, their early lives, their home, and their relationships to the area. A new Lincoln Presidential Museum and Library has recently opened, just a few blocks away. If one wants to immerse himself into Lincoln history, this town and the surrounding area are musts.

I was the first of several guides to report to duty that winter. Basically, I was to research, develop, and conduct tours of the Lincoln Home, taking a maximum of 15 people through the rooms on two floors, in about 12 to 15 minutes. The tour was to dwell on the man and his family, not so much the house that Lincoln owned but where he learned that he had been nominated as the Republican party's nominee for President of the United States.

I conducted 502 tours of the home that season for 6739 visitors. In addition, I worked at the beautiful visitor center, conducted tours for Springfield fifth graders, and spent an hour with those same fifth graders in a classroom conducting three activities after their tour of the house and the small museum. Like the Muir mobile, I developed one regarding Mr. Lincoln and used it in the classroom. A wonderful teacher from Enos School wrote, "The new language arts activities were great! It really appealed to the students & was a well thought out activity & quite worthwhile. I have brought my classes to Lincoln's Home for 13 years in a row & Ranger Boyer has been the best, the most informative, the friendliest, etc! I was impressed with his whole presentation."

Recalling this class and teacher, they were engaged, prepared, and disciplined, ready to learn as much as they could. Ah, a great day!!

We conducted tours for the general public and especially for eighth graders who were studying Lincoln and his life in Springfield. Sometimes those students could be a challenge, talking throughout the tour, touching everything in the house, and sometimes punching and shoving each other—all dependent on how in touch the teacher and parents were. Overall, I found them attentive, ready to learn, and a bit awestruck with Lincoln and his home. It was disconcerting one day as a precocious student jumped on the Lincoln bed. Peter, our law enforcement ranger, had a very serious chat about respect!

Opening and working at the Great Western Depot was inspirational as well. A few blocks from the Lincoln site, this allowed us to interpret this site where Lincoln gave his parting speech, afterwards heading to Washington to begin his presidency.

I found a wonderfully diverse group of people working at this site. Cat, Gene, Jim, and Matt were permanents who always were available for advice and help.

Visitors would arrive at the visitor center, get a free ticket to tour the home and perhaps watch the free movie about the site. Robert Lincoln, son of the president, had given the home to the state; later it became a NPS unit. Robert indicated in the agreement that a fee should never be charged for tours. Tours were offered, depending on the time of day, either fifteen minutes apart, ten minutes apart, or every five minutes. A guide would meet the groups outside the Lincoln Home, give them a short introduction, and then line them up in front of the house and escort them into the house, sometimes doing the tour as well.

The site provided a variety of experiences for the guide—working at the vc, doing the intros, conducting tours, teaching the children, manning the depot, or doing some research as I did with the learning goals. Although doing the tours sometimes became laborious, it was important to remember that each visitor might be experiencing this opportunity for the first time, or certainly hearing it from a different ranger. With the limited amount of time to go through the house, it was very important to give the best tour and message. Cat, Gene and fellow guides could always be counted on to commiserate, cooperate, and counsel.

My boss, Cat, asked that I contact the Illinois Office of Education and connect our educational activities with the State Goals for Learning. This took some time, but fortunately, I was granted a nice cash stipend and a Certificate of Achievement for accomplishing this relationship.

After having a class visit the site, we asked teachers to fill out an evaluation which yielded some very nice comments.

Overall, the experience was a very good one. I have the pleasure of continuing to communicate with some of my fellow guides who have moved on to other various jobs.

In June, I started back at Rocky for the summer season. A program which I continued was "Importance of Being a Beaver." Conducted at beautiful Hollowell Park, visitors were always interested in this animal—its habitat, its activities, and its wonderful help for other animals in the park and its ability to provide protection of wetlands.

Although limited in number, this versatile and smart animal intrigued us all—its dam building ability, its tree-felling capabilities, its canal building in order to move limbs and trees, and its wide tail, its webbed back feet, and its sleek pelt.

In September, I supervised the Elk Bugle Corps. This wonderful group of volunteers from all walks of life, about ten to 15 of them, go out each night in three areas of the park to interpret the elk, control traffic, give directions, stress safety, and assist with the elk rut watching. It is a dramatic time of the year with several hundred thousand visitors coming into Rocky to view the rut from about the first of September to the end of October. Each ranger gets to do a thirty minute program called "Elk Echoes" each night, either at the Moraine Park Museum Amphitheatre or at the Sheep Lakes area. Many visitors attend these programs, offered at 6 p.m. One elderly, little prim lady, beautifully dressed, wanted to know if the bulls enjoyed the mating. She asked this question in front of a large group. Taken aback, I said that I had not noticed them smiling when this takes place! The response got a good laugh from the group.

All volunteers whom I have met are absolutely fabulous, people oriented, trained, and willing to be outside in some adverse weather conditions, and have often been at this for several years. Most spend one night a week doing this, but some come more often.

Similar to the Bighorn Brigade, they are members of the only group like this in the world.

Working at the Fall River Visitor Center, allowed me to develop a new program, "Bear Necessities" which I have since expanded to an evening program. This developed from a thirty minute program and seemed to be well received by the audience as I gave them an initial bear test based on some flash cards, with "gummy" bears as prizes; act out a short story regarding the bear's shrinking habitat; and close with safety around black bears.

I submitted this program for product assessment, interpretive talk, to the Mather Training Center in early 2003, and three reviewers determined that this submission product "demonstrates the certification standards for this competency." Receiving this review by three permanent NPS interpreters, was helpful in knowing that I was in conjunction with the standards set by the NPS. I have continued to revise and lengthen the program, fitting it into the campground setting and time length.

A ranger never knows in what way a visitor might be influenced or impressed. A lady visitor from Loveland, OH wrote to the Superintendent in August, 2002, "On July 4, 2002, I brought my 6-year-old son into the ranger station with all the rocks he had collected on a trail in Rocky Mountain National Park. I knew he could not keep them, but my son insisted there was gold in the rocks.

I felt the best way for him to learn was to talk with a ranger. So we talked to Ranger Richard Boyer. He was really wonderful with my son. Then he looked at each rock with my son, and told him what kind of rocks my son had found. Then, in a spontaneous act of kindness, thoughtfulness and generosity, Mr. Boyer purchased the book, *Rocks and Minerals*, and gave it to my son. My son was thrilled! He read the entire book during the rest of the day. Mr. Boyer suggested we talk with Ranger George, a retired geologist who was at the Bighorn Sheep meadow. He talked with my son for a while about the rocks he had found, and then we returned the rocks. We want to thank you, Mr. Boyer and Ranger George for making our visit so special."

2003—REDWOOD NATIONAL AND STATE PARKS AND ROCKY MOUNTAIN NATIONAL PARK

THE PRE-SCHOOL CHALLENGE!

In March I experienced a different type of position in the NPS—as an education technician at Redwood National and State Parks in northern CA.

Describing Redwood National and State Parks can be difficult. Spanning several miles, north to south, some of the largest Redwoods exist in the world, many over 300 feet high, deeply ridged bark, somewhat soft, sometimes dropping a large branch, appropriately called a "widow maker."

To stand among these stately giants can be stimulating and awesome. To know that some of their canopies, containing micro-worlds of plants and animals, are unique in their beauty and their holding of life. Knowing the human history of harvesting these trees which existed before Congress approved its status as a National park—all experiences anyone can appreciate in this diverse, coastal park.

Often students, teachers, parents, and we rangers would simply sniff, touch, and view the redwoods, not saying or doing anything that might spoil the moment!

Boss Lynda was wonderful—caring, helpful, understanding, and had a wealth of information both in her head and in the education center where we did our preparation for schools that would be visiting the Howland Hills Education Center, about four miles away among the Redwood trees.

I researched, developed, and presented education resource/curriculum based units to pre-schoolers through sixth graders. Redwoods, salmon, tide pools, animals, plants, and stream studies were the units.

Lynda, myself, and two Student Conservation Association young men, Adam and Mike, would work Mondays through Fridays, generally with a different class each day, but sometimes the classes would stay for two or three days.

We would meet at the education center, pick up all of our supplies and head for the isolated, yet rustic and stimulating education center.

My initial connection with the class was to meet them at the bus parking lot and then escort them through the half mile "Unnatural Trail" where they would count the number of things that should NOT be on the trail—stuffed animals, colored bows, plastic toys to name a few. The trail to the center was about one-half mile long, and the students, teachers, parents, and I would wind up "sneaking" up on the others where we would loudly yell, "Surprise."

Then Mike or Adam would conduct a tour as I prepared for my first unit presentation. Usually we would get one or two units in before lunch, lunch, then a climb on the cut-off redwood stumps, a couple more units after lunch, or a hike out to the busses. The days always went fast as the students had to be back at school in order for the busses to begin their journeys home.

Monday might be fourth graders, followed on Tuesday by pre-schoolers, sixth graders on Wednesday, second graders on Thursday, and third graders on Friday, so a mind-shift had to take place each morning as well as having different materials. Pre-schoolers were indeed a challenge, finding out that the best method with them is to keep them moving about every twenty seconds—"Here is a redwood; now let's move on to these leaves; over here are some lizards; notice the birds; let's get to the burned out tree;"—it seemed to work!

Lynda made it fun as did Adam and Mike, two young men in their twenties who were excellent with the children and creative with their programs. It was a privilege to work with all three of them.

One short program I did was about gray whales which were migrating north and pretty close to the shore. I had just set up my props on an available picnic table along the shore, was "waxing" about the size and the migration when Mike stepped up and whispered in my ear, "There is one just behind you in the ocean!"

What timing!! Immediately, I said, "Now is the time to observe this beautiful animal." They all scurried closer to the ocean. We all followed, giving as much information as possible as she and her calf went slowly by, maybe less than 100 yards out. Of course, I took credit for her presence!

The summer season back at Rocky was a bit different as I worked intermittently only, due to some family responsibilities. But, there was considerable work offered, so I did programs on beaver, bears, wildlife, elk, and, of course, spent time behind the desk at four sites in the park.

Part of my time at Rocky has been working in the Information Office. It is a hub of information regarding anything in the park or anything going on in the park. A volunteer and I worked the phones, answering all kinds of questions, sending out materials, often to students, and the additional duty of answering emails.

We also took information from the dispatch office, such as road closures or campgrounds which had filled, and passed that information on to our visitor centers and to several outside-of-park agencies so they knew what is going on in the park. There are some interesting questions which come in by email or by phone. Some give us great laughs, but to the caller or emailer, it is important.

2004—REDWOOD NATIONAL AND STATE PARKS AND ROCKY MOUNTAIN NATIONAL PARK

THE SALAMANDER CATCH

Returning to Redwood for the spring season as education technician, was enjoyable again. Lynda was still my supervisor, and a new SCA, Sarah, was employed.

The state parks had acquired a new area with a beautiful stream and remnants of a wood mill. This added to what was available for students and teachers. I had the role of walking students about a half mile to the stream area, and conducting a stream study to determine how clean and effective the stream was for fish. Sometimes on the walk we observed big Roosevelt elk.

I also had, from the Howland Hills Ed Center, the opportunity to walk students in again and sometimes to walk them about two miles down through the old growth redwoods to a different stream for studies.

On the way, we would stop at several interpretative spots, my favorite being at one of the big redwoods where we would put everyone around the tree, and have students guess the circumference. Whoever got closest to that figure, received the "prized" candy bar.

One of the activities I really enjoyed, and it worked with any age, was to give each person a penny. They had thirty seconds to put as much nature on that penny as they could. It was always amazing to me what they would come up with. One parent stood on her penny. Another balanced a very long downed limb on his penny.

The point made was to indicate how much nature was in this park, how diverse it was, and to point out that this activity could be used anywhere—in their own back yards, or in other parks. I told them that this was their penny to keep and to remember where they were and what they were seeing when they next looked at their penny. Then, I also asked them, "a penny for your thoughts." Sometimes I would get a response. I have used this activity for "Kids Adventure" and other programs at Rocky.

Taking older children to the ocean tide pools was extremely rewarding, watching them in the tide pools, looking for creatures such as anemones and learning to understand how strong these creatures are, how the tides work, and winding up putting some type of message in the sand.

They could look down and see these messages as we worked our way back up the hill.

One enjoyable unit was introducing first-graders to the "Underworld," a take-off of what Michael had done the previous year. The unit was designed to show the children some of the invertebrates that live in the forest, including salamanders which might be found under a fallen tree.

One sweet, prim, neatly dressed little girl had been quiet, but very attentive as the unit was introduced. As we moved into the forest to "search" for some of the underworld animals, I turned over a fallen, decaying tree, revealing a nice sized salamander. She quickly moved to pick it up and show it to everyone as we identified it.

Her teacher and mother stood with their mouths open, saying that they could not believe she would have done that as she is pretty "prissy" when it comes to science and working with animals. The pride shown by the girl's standing tall is a memory I won't soon forget. It was a great moment for all of us!

This beautiful park, its resources and activities, have left some wonderful images to remember.

The summer was full-time seasonal at Rocky where I worked at four visitor centers.

"Becoming a Naturalist" was an interesting program conducted in beautiful Upper Beaver Meadows. The size of the group really varied so quick adaptations had to be made—fewer or more materials, longer or shorter—in order to move everyone, and perhaps louder to get messages across.

It was a program where visitors could be immersed in the resource, doing the frame activity, becoming cameras to take a closer look at nature, checking out quotes placed in the woods, and learning about the flora and fauna of the area. The two-hour program was fun to conduct, and often a beautiful blue bird would be at the trailhead, welcoming us back.

The "Lily Lake Wildflower Walk" was always fun, starting at beautiful Lily Lake parking lot. The size for this group varied, never knowing how many would show up and how knowledgeable they might be about flowers.

One very rainy afternoon, it was misting. About four people were present, and then I noticed about ten people approaching. A gentleman indicated that they were a group of botanists visiting from Canada. I took a big breath, and said, "Well, then you can help me with this program." They all laughed and said they were actually all ministers, staying at a nearby Conference Center. It was a good laugh for all and certainly some relief for the ranger! We started the walk and the rain came harder with some lightning. A few yards into the walk I indicated that the talk was over.

I think there was relief as many of them had no rain gear. We are always very aware of bad weather including lightning since CO is the second most struck state after Florida.

2005—POINT REYES NATIONAL SEASHORE AND ROCKY MOUNTAIN NATIONAL PARK

TWO DIVERSE "JEWELS"

Point Reyes National Seashore became my winter seasonal position, starting in March, lasting until early June. This beautiful, but diverse park, was wonderful. From the many coastal regions, featuring passing gray whales, elephant seals, varied bird species, and the soothing movement and sounds of the waves crashing, to the inland forested mountains, wildflowers, Tule elk, and numerous varied trails, this park also provides visitors a chance to experience nature at its finest. Its tallest peak, Mt. Wittenberg, with its beautiful trails and wildflowers, a variety of birds, deer, the ocean with all of its mysteries—all provided a setting that one could never fully assimilate.

About an hour Northwest of San Francisco, its history of the Miwok Native Americans, Sir Francis Drake, and the 1870 lighthouse make for an interesting visit, hopefully for more than one day.

Boss John, and several other great staff made it a wonderful experience.

The park guide position included half days at the Bear Valley Visitor Center followed by collateral duties and then some full days at the cliff side lighthouse, built in 1870.

Although the park was about an hour's drive from San Francisco, it was often not that busy, except on weekends. A variety of people visited—birders, animal lovers, wildflower experts, campers, hikers, bikers, all with their own agendas. Working at the visitor center, allowed me to interact with visitors, sell items, give information, send out materials, and answer phone calls. Usually one other staff member was present.

The Bear Valley VC is absolutely beautiful, not only in its setting in this varied weather valley, but also with its many exhibits—animals, weather, birds, and whales—an award winner!

Driving the Toyota Prius to the lighthouse was a 45 minute drive. The Prius was given to the park and had park scenery on both sides. The drive passed along a bay through a couple of small towns and on through cattle ranches, a part of the park.

The lighthouse site was small, yet had an informative visitor center, and the lighthouse, some 308 steps down to a point where the lighthouse was located and where whale watching was a prime activity.

I had to prepare a lighthouse presentation for the afternoon when the lighthouse was open to visitors. It was fascinating to present this information to the many visitors from all over the world. The lighthouse housing the large 1st order Fresnel lens—although no longer in operation—had been replaced by a modern light and foghorn. About three-hundred feet above the ocean standing on the platform next to the lighthouse, afforded wonderful views of the ocean, both north and south, and, of course, spectacular sunsets.

One of my activities, when not working at a visitor center, was roving the trails. So, I put together a photo album with pictures of many of the trails, describing them to visitors who had an interest

As usual, wonderful volunteers assisted at the visitor centers including Sally and Dee.

One day I received a call asking if a guide animal could be brought into the park. I said, "yes" but that it would help if the animal had an identification vest or if the person had some written ID regarding it being a guide dog. The caller, with this unrecognizable accent, said "No, no, it is a guide chimpanzee, and it was trained nearby." "Oh, I said, I am not sure, let me transfer you to our dispatch." The caller hung up, and there, about thirty feet away was a veteran ranger, John, laughing his head off. The prank had worked

I knew I had to get revenge, so I searched the net, finding and ordering a stuffed animal chimpanzee. When it arrived, my wife made an apron for it imprinted with "John's Guide Service," and we made the presentation early one morning before the vc opened. It was a big hit and has followed him to HI and back to Yellowstone. A little innocent fun can get you through the day.

I submitted a lighthouse presentation for certification purposes, but did not attain certification—more work needed.

In Rocky, the summer of 2005, I had the opportunity to do "The Majestic Elk," again, an evening program at the intimate Glacier Basin Campground amphitheatre.

A thirty-minute program "Little Critters of Moraine Park" was presented at the Moraine Park Museum. This is always fun to present, especially to the children who sit on the floor and learn about and touch the animals. Many were working on their junior ranger badges.

Sometimes roving the park trails becomes a part of our duties. It might be a half-day rove or a full-day rove. We are to provide information, present mini-talks about a specific topic, ask them if everything in the park is going OK—signs understandable and visible, how the trails are, what suggestions they might have for improvement. So many people respond favorable to seeing a ranger.

One lady said, "I am envious of you." I told her I was envious of myself. Others say they are glad to see us on the trails, and so very many say, "Thanks for taking care of our parks." Hopefully we continue roving as a personal contact with the visitor is almost always appreciated.

It was this summer in "Ballad of the Bighorn Sheep" that I introduced the concept of comparing the tools people use to the tools that the Bighorn Sheep use to survive—the hammer indicating strength; the pliers gripping as the sheep's hooves do; the cutting tool representing their teeth; the measuring tape indicating how they "measure up" to other animals; and the carrying case for the tools, a comparison to the sheep's coat. It seemed to make sense to the audience.

The most dramatic incident was the death of ranger Jeff Christensen which occurred on July 29th At Rocky. Jeff was a law enforcement ranger who died from injuries sustained in a fall while patrolling the backcountry. It took eight days for rescuers to find his body. The whole country was watching and hoping for the best. Press covered it by the scores while additional manpower was brought in from all over the country.

Our job at various visitor centers was to direct those involved to the correct person in the park, to insist to press that there would be a briefing whenever determined by the park, to explain generally to the inquiring public what was happening, and to keep everything operating as smoothly as possible. It was heart-wrenching to witness staff who were so involved, and to remain focused on helping visitors.

On a prayer card at his memorial service, Jeff was quoted as saying, "You know, if I ever die while at work in the mountains, do not cry for me because you will know that I died doing what I love. But if I die in a car accident on my way to an office job, then cry for me because you will know I was miserable and not doing what I loved." Indeed, it was a sad summer.

On August 12, I received a nice letter sent by Anna and LeNaye from Whites Creek, TN. LeNaye, the mother, wrote, "Dear Ranger Rick, Thank you for your kindness to our daughter and to all of the other children in your program. Anna is still wearing her badge every day. Maybe being a Ranger is in her future! (Her grandpa was a forest ranger.)" Anna wrote, "I love you Ranger Rick. Love, Anna"

This is what it is all about—making a difference and making that connection for the visitors.

2006—POINT REYES NATIONAL SEASHORE

Getting a chance to spend a longer time this winter at Point Reyes National Seashore, allowed me to get to know the resource more, get to know fellow staff more, and get to know the visitors and their needs more.

One of my highlights was to revise and to update the old junior ranger book at the lighthouse. With supervisor Steve's wonderful suggestions, insights, and directions, it became a reality about the week I left in May. The revision was updated to include materials and activities about elephant seals, gray whales, and the lighthouse. It seemed to be well accepted after several weeks of work and several revisions.

Duties this season included working at the beautiful lighthouse one or two days a week, working at the information desk at Bear Valley Visitor Center, and doing collateral duties of cleaning cars, the desk area, waysides, roving, and sending out materials as requested.

Some great volunteers were present to assist and add their knowledge. Selling association materials was another duty we performed. This happens in almost every setting, depending on the relationship of the park and the association. Splitting wood became another collateral duty which I truly enjoyed.

To have a nice fire burning in the vc stove helped warm the building but more importantly allowed another venue for visitors to relax, and ponder the beauties of nature through the center's windows. Often they could view a variety of birds, deer, the Morgan horses, and springtime flowers.

2006—ROCKY MOUNTAIN NATIONAL PARK

THE BEARS COME OUT

This summer was an intermittent one as several family activities were on tap although not taking away from several days of work in the park. Working at the various visitor centers, and doing talks/walks kept me busy enough. This was the first time that I had switched "Bear Necessities" from a short program into an evening program. Adding more information about bears including some research was enough to reach forty minutes.

2007—SAN FRANCISCO MARITIME NATIONAL HISTORICAL PARK AND ROCKY MOUNTAIN NATIONAL PARK

In late 2006, I was interviewed and hired for a park guide position at San Francisco Maritime National Historical Park but was delayed by the mandatory security check which came through in late January. I reported on February 4 after arriving in San Francisco on the 2nd. Kathy was my boss there, and the job involved fee collection, interpretation of this beautiful site, and working at visitor center desks. The site was on the Hyde Street Pier and had several historic ships docked and available for viewing. This was a detailed and fascinating area with views of the Golden Gate Bridge and Alcatraz. Unfortunately, because of a son's illness, I left the site after three days of work

I was, as usual, impressed by the staff, the site, and the possibility of learning much in a whole different type of setting. Hopefully, I can return there some day.

The summer of '07 at RMNP was my best schedule yet!! Having Sundays and Mondays off provided a respite from a busy weekend day and a chance to do personal business on Monday. Tuesday, the day started at 12:15 and ran until 9:15 with two programs on the agenda as well as some collateral duties—duties which are assigned by your supervisor—in my case, cleaning a park vehicle; running off the bi-weekly ranger schedule; and inspecting the plaza, restrooms, and walkways in front of the Beaver Meadows Visitor Center. Wednesday was spent at the Sheep Lakes Information Station, providing two talks about bighorn sheep and supervising four volunteers. Thursday was at Fall River Visitor Center, doing a story time program in the morning. Friday was a "rove" day, going into the park to rove the trails and provide information to park visitors. Saturday, two programs were presented, a "Dream Lake Hike" for two hours and "Kids Adventure" in the afternoon.

A wonderful experience happened on my "Dream Lake Hike" on Saturday, July 7. I had taken a family of four and two older ladies on the hike, arriving at Dream Lake around

11:00 a.m. I gave my usual conclusion and then presented John Muir's famous quote, "Climb the mountains and get their good tidings . . ."

An elderly lady who had not been on the tour tapped me on the shoulder and said, "I just love that quote, and my father is having it put on his tombstone." I asked her how old he was, and she said he had passed away on the preceding Tuesday and was 99. It was a sad moment, but a happy one, as she related how much he loved that quote. Then, she had me recite it to another lady—not sure if she was a friend or relative—and when I finished, this elderly lady also cried. It was an extremely touching moment. You had to be there with beautiful Dream Lake in the background, having a great bunch of six people on the walk, and then to have this touching scene unfold as not only she listened, but several others as well. These moments make this job rewarding!

On Wednesday, July 4, I was working at the Sheep Lakes Information Station, and it was about 2:45 p.m. A young man came to the station, and said that he had lost his car keys at the Lawn Lake Trailhead about a half mile away. He believed that he had lost them in the toilet, and that another man had probably picked them up and taken them. I checked with the entrance station, had ROMO check with the lost and found, and the Fall River Visitor Center. No one had seen them. We went back to the trailhead and looked again. He said he would stay there, hoping the man would come back. I told him we would leave at 4 p.m., if he needed further help. About 3:45, he arrived again. He had already hiked about 12 miles that day on some pretty steep terrain, so was tired

One of our volunteers agreed to take him to the Fall River VC where he could call one of his friends to bring up some other keys—he was also going to be late to his delivery job which started in Boulder at 5 p.m.

As I left, I decided to check back at the trailhead to see if the keys might have been posted somewhere. They were not. Then I called on one of my favorite saints, St. Anthony, patron of lost items. I told him that this young man seemed nice, and it would be great if I could locate the keys. As I approached his car, looking under and into it, I checked the roof, and there on top were the keys, just where he had put them. I radioed ROMO and asked them to call the Fall River VC to let the man know I had found the keys, and that I would take them there. He, indeed, was relieved, but embarrassed that he had blamed someone else for taking them, but had inadvertently left them on top of his own car. He said he would probably be one of those visitors who would be talked about in the future—not much, of course!

A nice surprise arrived soon after my season ended on August 18. Dated September 02, was the STAR AWARD which was signed by the park superintendent. His letter accompanying the award read, "It is my pleasure to award you $100.00, and my thanks, for consistently performing at a level above the requirements for your position and grade. Your themes, goals and objectives reflect carefully planned and organized efforts in each interpretive program

Universal concepts are evident and clearly developed in all interpretive programs. Your programs are relevant and meaningful to audiences no matter what the age or background. Your professionalism, sincerity, approachability and obvious love for the resource make you an ideal National Park Service Representative." A nice way to end the season!! Most of the seasonals also received this award.

In early November, my boss, Sue, indicated that my program, "Ballad of the Bighorn Sheep," which had been submitted to the Mather Training Center as an example of an interpretive talk, had been found to "demonstrate the certification standards for this competency." It sure helps to know that what you are doing seems to be in the right direction as determined by two permanent park service certifiers.

2008—ROCKY MOUNTAIN NATIONAL PARK

A WINTER EXPERIENCE

This was my first winter season to have the opportunity to work full-time at Rocky Mountain National Park, starting on February 3, ending April 12th.

Work included doing two programs, "Skins and Skulls," a Saturday afternoon thirty-minute talk, and a two-hour snowshoe walk on Mondays from 12:30 to 2:30 p.m. starting at Bear Lake.

Staffing the visitor center desks at Beaver Meadows Visitor Center and Fall River Visitor Center and doing collateral duties comprised the forty hour week.

Conducting the beginning snowshoe/ecology walks each week was so rewarding—watching visitors get ready, informing them about the walk, introducing them to the area and to the volunteer who assisted, and then moving them into some new territory.

On one walk, volunteer Jim was at the back of the group just up from the beginning of the steeper fire trail, when a grandfather, accompanied by his wife and two grandsons, became ill. Jim radioed that he was taking the group back to their car as the man seemed to be dizzy and was sitting down on the snow. I radioed him, asking if the man were having any chest pain; Jim said that he was not.

So, I continued with the rest of the group as Jim took them back to their car. I later called the wife, and she said that her husband was doing fine, and she appreciated the call.

Later the park received a nice thank-you letter indicating, "Dear Ranger Rick and Volunteer Jim, Our family would like to thank you for your extreme kindness and concern when we were snowshoeing on Monday, February 11. Bill ended up with fever and chills and flu-like intestinal symptoms. He must have picked up a bug on our travels.

He is now about 90% recovered. The fever would explain his very red face which was puzzling to me. We felt very safe and well provided for. We were grateful for the help especially because our grandchildren were with us. They told their mom that Ranger Rick even called us to check on us. They have a wonderful memory of the two very kind rangers. Sincerely, Bill and Sue"

"Ranger Rick" was a name I had starting using about three or four years ago, but the receivers of the letter at the park did not know who Ranger Rick was, so it became a mission for them to figure out who this was. Finally, this unknown ranger was identified. And the letter was read to an all-park meeting and Ranger Rick became a reality!!

Sometimes we get to give programs, not normally scheduled and not in the park.

On February 12, it was fun to present a program to ten first, second, and third grade boys at the Estes Park Library. They belong to a book club and meet weekly. The boys seemed to enjoy the twenty-five scat and tracks program. Kerry and Melanie, leaders of the program, wrote, "Dear Richard, Thank you so much for sharing your knowledge about scat and animal tracks at our book club meeting last Tuesday. The 1st, 2nd & 3rd grade boys were mesmerized. You were such an excellent presenter, and it was very evident that you had a teaching background. We'd love to have you visit our library another time. You were great!!"

SUMMER, 2008—ROCKY MOUNTAIN NATIONAL PARK

It happened twice during the season—a small girl's hand slipping into mine during "Kids' Adventure," a program offered each Saturday afternoon at beautiful Sprague Lake. It happened near the end of the program, both girls about five or six years old. As we headed toward the river from doing the "framing" exercise, it was startling at first to have a small hand slip into mine—one of those special moments, always checking with a parent to see if this is acceptable.

On a beautiful, sunny day while roving at Alluvial Fan, a beaming, smiling lady was coming down the short trail after experiencing the falls and the beauty of the area. She stopped as she saw me approaching, raised both hands, looking toward the sky and said, "That just opens your heart!" What an inspiring statement!! It took me by surprise, but as I discussed the moment with my supervisor, it was obvious that she had captured the magic and the beauty of Rocky in this experience.

Obviously we cannot take tips for presentations, but it is always nice for visitors to offer one. Often at the end of the "Dream Lake Hike," visitors would offer one. It was rewarding to have that offer, but I would tell them that they could make a donation at one of our visitors' centers.

Rocky has a sister park in Poland, and it was my honor to accompany five employees from that park as they visited. My task was to take them up the Bear Lake corridor with stops at Sprague Lake and a tour around Bear Lake. The guests were so intrigued with the views and could not stop taking pictures.

In mid-October, I had another special tour, with Roxanne Quimby, a philanthropist, who has been a supporter of national parks, especially Acadia National Park in Maine. She developed the Burt's Bees products and was visiting the area in conjunction with a presentation she was making in CO. She, her daughter and her daughter's boyfriend, arrived about 10:45 a.m. at the Beaver Meadows Visitor Center.

They were amazed at the beauty of the park as I took them up Trail Ridge Road, stopping at several over-looks for pictures and information. At the Forest Canyon overlook, the clouds were below us in the canyon with beautiful sunshine above.

On October 14, she sent a book and nice thank-you note reading, "Hi Dick! *Many many* thanks for the awesome tour of Rocky Mt. NP!! *So* cool—we loved the views & invigorating atmosphere. You are so generous with your time & we certainly appreciated it. Hope to see you again."

Each summer and sometimes during the other seasons, the park has interns and other volunteers working in our division. Because of the number of applicants, we get some wonderful young people, eager to learn, not only about the park, but also about interpreting it.

One such intern this summer was Tyler. He had come by bus from New York state to immerse himself in the area and in interpretation. He did an excellent job with glowing reports from visitors.

At the end of his season, in August, I bought him a shirt with Rocky Mountain scenes on it. He wrote a touching note, "You gave me a shirt on Thursday, but in doing so you have given me a relic of the passionate people and enduring landscape that will forever color and clothe my remembrance of this time and this place. It is a most generous gift, and for it I am forever indebted." What a joy to work with.

In the middle of July at my evening program, "The Bear Facts," a family had requested a sign language interpreter. This was new to me, so as Mark, the sign language interpreter arrived, he told me to do as I usually do, and that he would stand behind me about ten feet to my right. I actually could not see his signing, but the family was truly happy with his efforts. It was another "notch" in experiences as a park ranger.

2009—POINT REYES NATIONAL SEASHORE

This became my third season at this beautiful 71,000 acre seashore. Duties included working at the Bear Valley Visitor Center, roving, doing assigned projects, and working one or two days a week at the lighthouse.

One of the rewarding experiences working at PORE, was getting the chance to be at the Bear Valley trailhead, giving out information to visitors—maps, current flowers blooming, distances, difficulties, and answering questions. Visitors really enjoyed seeing a ranger "out in the field."

Another enjoyable part of this season was the housing assigned. It was a two bedroom, two bath room, about ¼ mile walking distance to the Bear Valley Visitor Center. Although a bit dirty when I arrived, it was very roomy with a nice kitchen and a very small television which could only get three stations—but who is counting? I was supposed to share with an intermittent researcher on occasion, but he never did show up while I was there.

Aaron and Christy, friends of my daughter, visited twice and my daughter Mary and granddaughter Mackenzie visited with them once. We got a free fire permit for an evening fire on the beach and watched the Pacific sunset twice as we cooked foil wraps. A drive to the beach and the sunset fire, enjoying family and friends, are some of perks of working in a National Park Service unit.

Being close to a large metropolitan area gave me a chance to visit San Francisco, Santa Rosa, and other interesting areas. Being an avid bicyclist, I road across the Golden Gate bridge twice to the quaint town of Sausalito. Riding the ferry from near San Rafael to San Francisco is always fun, watching the other people, many businessmen, viewing Alcatraz, and seeing other ships and boats.

A variety of stores are in the area, including many health food stores in the small town of Point Reyes. Although more expensive, organic food is plentiful in the area.

2009—ROCKY MOUNTAIN NATIONAL PARK

Due to some family obligations this summer, I only worked intermittently during the first part of this season. Because of the departure of one ranger and two others wanting to leave early, I began seasonally full-time in late August.

I presented the bighorn sheep program several times this summer, usually twice each day, and had the opportunity to see the bighorn, symbol of Rocky and state mammal of CO. The four volunteers, members of the Bighorn Brigade, were always a joy to work with. Rocky, boasting almost 2,000 volunteers, has this particular group coming to the Sheep Lakes area to assist answering questions, keep people away from the sheep, and direct traffic when the sheep cross busy US highway 34. A diverse group of people, from all walks of life, some retired, they bring that special quality of wanting to volunteer in a national park unit.

My evening program, "Bear Necessities" was presented several times, both at the Moraine Park Campground amphitheatre and at the Beaver Meadows Visitor Center.

Being inter-active, it is fun to do, especially quizzing the visitors about black bears, and awarding gummy bears to the person with the correct answers. One of the audience members gets the chance to deliver the gummy bears, getting any that are left. They love it!

One evening, about two-thirds of the way through this program, a member of the audience, sitting at the back of the theatre, began yelling very loudly that I was wrong with the information given about fighting back if a black bear were ever to attack you, which is rare. He went on for about two or three minutes which seemed an eternity! I just let him yell loudly at me while not knowing what to do never having had this happen before. He was a local, who had been attacked by a black bear, and he knew I was giving the wrong information. After his tirade, indicating to him that this was not the information I had read and learned, but that he could see me after the program. Indeed, he did come up and began to yell at me again. Finally I asked, "Who are you?" He shook his hand at me and left. The audience was shocked as I was, and several of them told me that they thought that the situation was handled well. I fully expected to see a letter to the local newspaper indicating what this "dumb" ranger was telling everyone.

After further research from supervisors, pamphlets put out by the park service and the CO Division of Wildlife, and other publications, it was obvious to me he did not know what he was talking about. Whew!!

This fall, my schedule became full-time. The "Bear Lake Stroll," "Elk Echoes," "Here Come the Beetles," and the "Moraine Park Nature Walk" were programs that I was able to do. Also, were several days of working at the Beaver Meadows Visitor Center info desk and at the beautiful Moraine Park Visitor Center.

The "Bear Lake Stroll." an hour-long stroll around the lake, was enjoyable, relaxing with a variety of people. Because the trail is so busy, logistically, it is a bit of a challenge. Informing visitors of the human and geological history, the flora and fauna, and answering their questions were really fun. Getting around the lake in one-hour while trying to be inspiring and informative was a challenge.

Because of many of our lodgepole pines, ponderosa, and some spruce being attacked by the pine beetle in recent years, a new program was presented, "Here Come the Beetles." As visitors could view, many of the trees had been infested. It was my job in this presentation to inform about the history of the beetle, what the park was doing to mitigate the problem, and what the future might bring. So visible to the public, it was probably the most asked about subject during this season.

The fall season always brings the elk "rut," a Latin word meaning "to roar." It is the mating season for these majestic animals, running from about mid-September to mid-October—the time of the year when the bulls form "harems" (herds) of about 15 to 20 females per bull.

The "bugle," from the bull lets the cow know which one is most mature, and warns lesser bulls. The bulls keep their herds together, ward off other bulls of lesser stature, and generally provide a wonderful viewing time for the hundreds of thousands who come to watch this ritual.

Not always knowing what duty might be assigned, my supervisor Sue along with Public Information Officer, Kyle, asked me to do some public service radio spots for a local FM station. I was to develop about six of these, clear them with my supervisor and then record them at the station. Wildlife, Things to Do, Visitor Center Hours and Programs, and Autumn Colors and Wildlife were the spots to be presented.

Although another enjoyable experience, I am not sure how often they were aired, having only heard one spot myself.

As always, it was sad for me as the final day, October 11th, arrived.

CONCLUSION

It is my hope that this book has offered anyone interested the chance to "taste" the rewards and challenges of working seasonally as an interpretative park ranger for the National Park Service. Without actually working in the service, it is difficult to present how one can truly experience the mostly joys and a few sorrows.

I am not sure who wrote the following, but it sums up my feelings toward this inspiring work.

"WHEN GOD CREATED RANGERS"

When the good Lord was creating rangers, He was into His 5th day of overtime when an angel appeared and said, "You're doing a lot of fiddling around on this one." The Lord said, "Have you read the specs on this order? The ranger has to be completely washable, but not plastic—have 180 moving parts, all replaceable—run on black coffee and leftovers—have a smile that won't quit—a manner that cures anything from a broken leg to a disappointed trail hiker—and six pairs of hands." The angel shook her head slowly and said, "Six pairs of hands? No way." "It's not the hands that are causing me problems," said the Lord. "It's the three pairs of eyes that rangers must have." "That's on the standard mode?" asked the angel.

The Lord nodded. "One pair that sees thru closed doors when the ranger asks, "What do you visitors see in the park?" when she already knows. Another in the back of her head that sees what she shouldn't see, but knows what she has to know. And, of course, the ones in front that can look at a visitor or staff member when they goof up and say, 'I understand and love, you,' without saying a word." "Lord said the angel, touching His sleeve gently, "go to bed. Tomorrow is another day." "I can't," said the Lord, "I'm so close now. Already I have one who heals herself when she is sick, can interpret the park on a moment's notice, and can sympathize and empathize with visitors and staff alike." The angel circled the model of the ranger very slowly. "It's too soft," she sighed.

"But tough," the Lord said excitedly. "You cannot imagine what this ranger can do or endure." "Can it think?" "Not only think, but it can reason and compromise," said the Lord. Finally, the angel bent over and ran her finger across the cheek. "There is a leak," she pronounced. "It's for joy, sadness, disappointment, pain, loneliness and pride." "You are a genius," said the angel. The Lord looked somber, "I didn't put it there."

CPSIA information can be obtained at www.ICGtesting.com
Printed in the USA
LVOW12s0734160414

381883LV00001B/91/P